50 French Appetizer Recipes for Home

By: Kelly Johnson

Table of Contents

- French Onion Soup Bites
- Gougères (Cheese Puffs)
- Croque-Monsieur Bites
- Escargot in Garlic Butter
- Ratatouille Tartlets
- Salmon Rillettes
- Quiche Lorraine Bites
- Coquilles St. Jacques (Scallops in Shell)
- Pissaladière (French Onion Tart)
- Mushroom Duxelles Crostini
- Salade Niçoise Skewers
- Brandade de Morue (Salt Cod Spread)
- Tarte Flambée (Alsatian Pizza)
- Brie and Pear Tartlets
- Foie Gras Mousse with Fig Jam
- Stuffed Mushrooms with Boursin Cheese
- Potato Leek Soup Shooters
- Smoked Salmon Canapés
- Pâté de Campagne (Country Pâté)
- Caramelized Onion and Bacon Tartlets
- Chicken Liver Pâté with Cornichons
- Provençal Tomato Tart
- Shrimp Cocktail with Sauce Marie Rose
- Mushroom and Gruyère Tartlets
- Crab Stuffed Mushrooms
- Fougasse (French Flatbread)
- Duck Rillettes
- Goat Cheese and Herb Stuffed Cherry Tomatoes
- Tartine with Tapenade and Anchovies
- Pork Rillettes
- Scallop and Bacon Skewers
- Mini Croque-Madame
- Endive Spears with Blue Cheese and Walnuts
- Tarte Tatin Bites (Upside-Down Apple Tart)
- Asparagus Wrapped in Prosciutto

- Mussels in White Wine Sauce
- Pissaladière Bites (Mini French Onion Tart)
- Chicken Liver Crostini with Caramelized Onions
- Mini Quiche Lorraine
- Tuna Tartare with Avocado
- Cherry Tomato and Mozzarella Skewers
- Duck Confit Crostini with Cherry Compote
- Smoked Salmon Blinis
- Cheese and Herb Soufflés
- Bouillabaisse Shooters
- Mushroom and Leek Quiche
- Chicken Liver Mousse with Port Wine Gelée
- Sardine Pâté on Baguette
- Cucumber Cups with Crab Salad
- Salmon Tartare with Dill and Capers

French Onion Soup Bites

Ingredients:

- 1 tablespoon olive oil
- 1 large onion, thinly sliced
- 1 teaspoon sugar
- 1 tablespoon balsamic vinegar (optional)
- Salt and pepper to taste
- 1 sheet of puff pastry, thawed
- 1 cup shredded Gruyère or Swiss cheese
- Fresh thyme leaves for garnish (optional)

Instructions:

1. Preheat your oven to 400°F (200°C). Line a baking sheet with parchment paper or a silicone baking mat.
2. In a large skillet, heat the olive oil over medium heat. Add the thinly sliced onion to the skillet and cook, stirring occasionally, until the onion is soft and caramelized, about 20-25 minutes.
3. Sprinkle the sugar over the caramelized onions and stir to combine. This helps to enhance the caramelization process. If using, add the balsamic vinegar to the skillet and cook for an additional 1-2 minutes, stirring to coat the onions evenly. Season with salt and pepper to taste.
4. Roll out the thawed puff pastry on a lightly floured surface into a large rectangle. Cut the puff pastry into small squares or rectangles, about 2x2 inches in size.
5. Transfer the puff pastry squares to the prepared baking sheet. Top each square with a spoonful of caramelized onions, then sprinkle shredded Gruyère or Swiss cheese over the onions.
6. Bake the French Onion Soup Bites in the preheated oven for 12-15 minutes, or until the puff pastry is golden brown and the cheese is melted and bubbly.
7. Remove the baking sheet from the oven and let the French Onion Soup Bites cool slightly. Garnish with fresh thyme leaves, if desired, before serving.
8. Serve the French Onion Soup Bites warm as a delicious appetizer for parties, gatherings, or as a tasty snack.

Enjoy the rich and savory flavors of French onion soup in these delightful bite-sized treats! They're sure to be a hit with family and friends.

Gougères (Cheese Puffs)

Ingredients:

- 1/2 cup (120ml) water
- 1/2 cup (120ml) whole milk
- 1/2 cup (115g) unsalted butter, cut into small pieces
- 1/2 teaspoon salt
- 1 cup (120g) all-purpose flour
- 4 large eggs
- 1 1/2 cups (150g) grated Gruyère cheese (or similar cheese such as Emmental or Comté)
- Freshly ground black pepper, to taste
- Pinch of nutmeg (optional)
- Egg wash (1 egg beaten with 1 tablespoon water), for brushing
- Additional grated cheese and/or flaky sea salt for topping (optional)

Instructions:

1. Preheat your oven to 425°F (220°C). Line a baking sheet with parchment paper or silicone baking mat.
2. In a medium saucepan, combine the water, milk, butter, and salt. Bring to a gentle boil over medium heat, stirring occasionally.
3. Once the mixture reaches a boil, reduce the heat to low and add the flour all at once. Stir vigorously with a wooden spoon until the mixture forms a smooth dough and pulls away from the sides of the pan, about 1-2 minutes.
4. Remove the saucepan from the heat and let the dough cool for a few minutes.
5. Add the eggs, one at a time, beating well after each addition, until the dough is smooth and glossy. The dough should be thick but still able to pipe.
6. Stir in the grated Gruyère cheese, black pepper, and nutmeg (if using), until evenly combined.
7. Transfer the dough to a piping bag fitted with a large round tip, or use a spoon to drop small mounds of dough onto the prepared baking sheet, leaving space between each puff.
8. Brush the tops of the Gougères with egg wash, and sprinkle with additional grated cheese and/or flaky sea salt, if desired.

9. Bake in the preheated oven for 15-20 minutes, or until the Gougères are puffed up, golden brown, and crispy.
10. Remove from the oven and let cool slightly before serving.
11. Serve the Gougères warm or at room temperature as a delicious appetizer or snack.

Enjoy these delightful cheese puffs with their light, airy texture and rich cheesy flavor.

They're perfect for entertaining or as a special treat for any occasion!

Croque-Monsieur Bites

Ingredients:

- 8 slices of sandwich bread (white or whole wheat)
- 4 tablespoons unsalted butter, softened
- 4 tablespoons all-purpose flour
- 1 cup whole milk
- 1/2 cup grated Gruyère cheese
- 1/4 cup grated Parmesan cheese
- 1/4 teaspoon nutmeg
- Salt and pepper to taste
- 8 slices of ham
- Dijon mustard, for spreading
- Fresh chives or parsley, finely chopped (for garnish, optional)

Instructions:

1. Preheat your oven to 375°F (190°C). Line a baking sheet with parchment paper.
2. Using a rolling pin, flatten each slice of bread until thin. Trim the crusts from the flattened bread slices.
3. Spread a thin layer of Dijon mustard on each slice of flattened bread.
4. Place a slice of ham on top of each bread slice.
5. In a small saucepan, melt 2 tablespoons of butter over medium heat. Add the flour and whisk continuously until the mixture is smooth and bubbling, about 1 minute.
6. Gradually pour in the milk while whisking constantly to prevent lumps from forming. Cook the sauce until thickened, about 3-4 minutes.
7. Remove the saucepan from the heat and stir in the grated Gruyère and Parmesan cheeses until melted and smooth. Season with nutmeg, salt, and pepper to taste.
8. Spread a layer of the cheese sauce over each slice of ham.
9. Roll up each slice of bread tightly, starting from one end, to form a pinwheel.
10. Place the pinwheels seam-side down on the prepared baking sheet.
11. Melt the remaining 2 tablespoons of butter and brush it over the tops of the pinwheels.
12. Bake in the preheated oven for 12-15 minutes, or until the Croque-Monsieur Bites are golden brown and crispy.

13. Remove from the oven and let cool slightly before serving.
14. Optionally, garnish with finely chopped fresh chives or parsley before serving.

Enjoy these delicious Croque-Monsieur Bites as a flavorful appetizer or snack, perfect for parties, brunches, or anytime you're craving a taste of France!

Escargot in Garlic Butter

1. Preheat your oven to 400°F (200°C).
2. In a small mixing bowl, combine the softened butter, minced garlic, chopped parsley, chopped thyme, salt, and black pepper. Mix until well combined.
3. Place a small amount of the garlic herb butter in each well of an escargot plate or a small oven-proof dish.
4. Place one escargot in each well on top of the garlic herb butter.
5. Spoon additional garlic herb butter over the top of each escargot, covering them generously.
6. Place the escargot plate or dish in the preheated oven and bake for 8-10 minutes, or until the butter is melted and bubbling.
7. While the escargot are baking, slice the baguette or French bread into thin slices and toast them lightly in the oven or under the broiler.
8. Once the escargot are cooked, remove them from the oven and let them cool slightly before serving.
9. Serve the Escargot in Garlic Butter hot, with the toasted baguette slices on the side for dipping into the flavorful butter sauce.
10. Optionally, garnish with additional chopped parsley or a squeeze of fresh lemon juice before serving.

Enjoy this elegant and flavorful French appetizer as a delicious start to any meal or as a special treat for a dinner party or celebration!

Ratatouille Tartlets

Ingredients:

- 1 can (about 7.5 ounces or 212g) escargot (canned or frozen), drained
- 1/2 cup (115g) unsalted butter, softened
- 3 cloves garlic, minced
- 2 tablespoons chopped fresh parsley
- 1 tablespoon chopped fresh thyme (or 1 teaspoon dried thyme)
- Salt and freshly ground black pepper, to taste
- Baguette or French bread, for serving

Instructions:

1. Preheat your oven to 400°F (200°C).
2. In a small mixing bowl, combine the softened butter, minced garlic, chopped parsley, chopped thyme, salt, and black pepper. Mix until well combined.
3. Place a small amount of the garlic herb butter in each well of an escargot plate or a small oven-proof dish.
4. Place one escargot in each well on top of the garlic herb butter.
5. Spoon additional garlic herb butter over the top of each escargot, covering them generously.
6. Place the escargot plate or dish in the preheated oven and bake for 8-10 minutes, or until the butter is melted and bubbling.
7. While the escargot are baking, slice the baguette or French bread into thin slices and toast them lightly in the oven or under the broiler.
8. Once the escargot are cooked, remove them from the oven and let them cool slightly before serving.
9. Serve the Escargot in Garlic Butter hot, with the toasted baguette slices on the side for dipping into the flavorful butter sauce.
10. Optionally, garnish with additional chopped parsley or a squeeze of fresh lemon juice before serving.

Enjoy this elegant and flavorful French appetizer as a delicious start to any meal or as a special treat for a dinner party or celebration!

Salmon Rillettes

Ingredients:

- 8 ounces (about 225g) smoked salmon or poached salmon, skin removed
- 4 ounces (about 115g) cream cheese, softened
- 2 tablespoons unsalted butter, softened
- 1 tablespoon lemon juice
- 1 tablespoon chopped fresh dill
- 1 tablespoon chopped fresh chives
- 1 teaspoon Dijon mustard
- Salt and freshly ground black pepper, to taste
- Toasted bread or crackers, for serving

Instructions:

1. If using smoked salmon, chop it finely. If using poached salmon, flake it into small pieces.
2. In a mixing bowl, combine the softened cream cheese, softened butter, and lemon juice. Mix until smooth and well combined.
3. Add the chopped salmon, chopped fresh dill, chopped fresh chives, Dijon mustard, salt, and black pepper to the bowl with the cream cheese mixture.
4. Stir everything together until evenly combined, but be careful not to overmix, as you want to maintain some texture.
5. Taste the salmon rillettes and adjust the seasoning if needed, adding more salt, pepper, or lemon juice to taste.
6. Transfer the salmon rillettes to a serving dish or individual ramekins.
7. Cover the dish or ramekins with plastic wrap and refrigerate for at least 1 hour to allow the flavors to meld together and the rillettes to firm up slightly.
8. When ready to serve, remove the salmon rillettes from the refrigerator and let them sit at room temperature for about 10-15 minutes to soften slightly.
9. Serve the salmon rillettes with toasted bread or crackers on the side for spreading.
10. Optionally, garnish the salmon rillettes with additional fresh herbs or a slice of lemon before serving.

Enjoy these creamy and flavorful salmon rillettes as a delightful appetizer for brunch, parties, or any occasion! They're sure to impress your guests with their elegant presentation and delicious taste.

Quiche Lorraine Bites

Ingredients:

For the pastry crust:

- 1 1/4 cups (155g) all-purpose flour
- 1/2 teaspoon salt
- 1/2 cup (115g) unsalted butter, cold and cut into small cubes
- 2-3 tablespoons ice water

For the filling:

- 4 slices bacon, cooked until crisp and crumbled
- 1/2 cup (50g) grated Gruyère or Swiss cheese
- 1/4 cup (60ml) heavy cream
- 1/4 cup (60ml) whole milk
- 2 large eggs
- Salt and freshly ground black pepper, to taste
- 1/4 cup (about 25g) chopped green onions or chives

Instructions:

1. Preheat your oven to 375°F (190°C). Grease a mini muffin tin or line it with mini muffin liners.
2. In a large mixing bowl, combine the flour and salt. Add the cold, cubed butter to the flour mixture.
3. Using a pastry blender or your fingertips, cut the butter into the flour until the mixture resembles coarse crumbs with some pea-sized pieces of butter remaining.
4. Add the ice water, one tablespoon at a time, tossing the mixture with a fork until the dough comes together and forms a rough ball. Be careful not to overwork the dough.
5. Turn the dough out onto a lightly floured surface and gently knead it a few times to bring it together. Shape the dough into a disk, wrap it in plastic wrap, and refrigerate for at least 30 minutes.

6. Once chilled, roll out the dough on a lightly floured surface to about 1/8 inch thickness. Using a round cookie cutter or glass, cut out circles of dough slightly larger than the wells of the mini muffin tin.
7. Press the dough circles into the wells of the mini muffin tin, pressing gently to adhere and form small pastry cups.
8. In a small bowl, whisk together the heavy cream, whole milk, eggs, salt, and pepper until well combined.
9. Divide the crumbled bacon, grated cheese, and chopped green onions evenly among the pastry cups.
10. Pour the egg mixture over the bacon, cheese, and green onions in each pastry cup, filling them almost to the top.
11. Bake in the preheated oven for 12-15 minutes, or until the quiche bites are puffed up and golden brown on top.
12. Remove from the oven and let cool in the muffin tin for a few minutes before carefully transferring the quiche bites to a wire rack to cool completely.
13. Serve the Quiche Lorraine Bites warm or at room temperature as a delicious appetizer or snack.

Enjoy these tasty and savory Quiche Lorraine Bites, perfect for brunch, parties, or any occasion!

Coquilles St. Jacques (Scallops in Shell)

Ingredients:

- 8 large scallops, preferably in their shells (if not available, use ramekins)
- 2 tablespoons unsalted butter
- 2 shallots, finely chopped
- 2 cloves garlic, minced
- 1/4 cup dry white wine
- 1/2 cup heavy cream
- 1 tablespoon chopped fresh parsley
- Salt and freshly ground black pepper, to taste
- 1/4 cup grated Gruyère or Parmesan cheese
- 1/4 cup breadcrumbs
- Lemon wedges, for serving
- Fresh parsley, for garnish (optional)

Instructions:

1. If using scallops in their shells, scrub the shells clean and remove the scallops. Rinse and dry the shells, then set them aside. If using ramekins, grease them lightly with butter and set aside.
2. Preheat your oven's broiler.
3. In a large skillet, melt the butter over medium heat. Add the chopped shallots and minced garlic, and sauté until softened and fragrant, about 2-3 minutes.
4. Add the scallops to the skillet and sear them on each side until golden brown, about 1-2 minutes per side. Remove the scallops from the skillet and set them aside.
5. Deglaze the skillet with white wine, scraping up any browned bits from the bottom of the pan. Let the wine reduce for a minute or two.
6. Stir in the heavy cream and chopped parsley. Season with salt and pepper to taste.
7. Place the scallops back into the skillet, spooning some of the cream sauce over each scallop.
8. If using scallop shells, arrange them on a baking sheet. If using ramekins, place them on the baking sheet.

9. In a small bowl, mix together the grated cheese and breadcrumbs. Sprinkle the mixture evenly over each scallop.
10. Place the baking sheet under the broiler and broil for 2-3 minutes, or until the cheese is melted and golden brown.
11. Remove from the oven and let the Coquilles St. Jacques cool slightly before serving.
12. Serve the Coquilles St. Jacques hot, garnished with fresh parsley and lemon wedges on the side.

Enjoy these elegant and flavorful Coquilles St. Jacques as a decadent appetizer or a main course for a special dinner!

Pissaladière (French Onion Tart)

Ingredients:

For the dough:

- 2 cups (250g) all-purpose flour
- 1 teaspoon salt
- 1 teaspoon sugar
- 1 packet (7g) instant yeast
- 3/4 cup (180ml) warm water
- 2 tablespoons olive oil

For the topping:

- 4 large onions, thinly sliced
- 2 tablespoons olive oil
- 2 cloves garlic, minced
- 1 teaspoon dried thyme
- Salt and freshly ground black pepper, to taste
- 1/2 cup (100g) black olives, pitted and halved
- 6-8 anchovy fillets (optional)
- Fresh thyme leaves, for garnish (optional)

Instructions:

1. In a large mixing bowl, combine the flour, salt, sugar, and instant yeast. Gradually add the warm water and olive oil, stirring until a dough forms.
2. Turn the dough out onto a lightly floured surface and knead it for about 5-7 minutes, or until smooth and elastic. Shape the dough into a ball.
3. Place the dough in a lightly oiled bowl, cover it with a clean kitchen towel or plastic wrap, and let it rise in a warm, draft-free place for about 1 hour, or until doubled in size.

4. While the dough is rising, prepare the topping. Heat the olive oil in a large skillet over medium heat. Add the thinly sliced onions and cook, stirring occasionally, until they are soft and caramelized, about 25-30 minutes.
5. Stir in the minced garlic and dried thyme, and cook for an additional 2-3 minutes. Season with salt and pepper to taste. Remove the skillet from the heat and let the onion mixture cool slightly.
6. Preheat your oven to 400°F (200°C). Line a baking sheet with parchment paper.
7. Once the dough has risen, punch it down and roll it out on a lightly floured surface into a rectangle or oval shape, about 1/4 inch thick. Transfer the rolled-out dough to the prepared baking sheet.
8. Spread the caramelized onion mixture evenly over the dough, leaving a small border around the edges.
9. Arrange the halved black olives and anchovy fillets (if using) on top of the onion mixture in a decorative pattern.
10. Bake the Pissaladière in the preheated oven for 20-25 minutes, or until the crust is golden brown and crispy.
11. Remove from the oven and let the Pissaladière cool slightly before serving.
12. Optionally, garnish with fresh thyme leaves before serving.

Enjoy this flavorful and savory Pissaladière as a delicious appetizer, snack, or light meal, perfect for sharing with family and friends!

Mushroom Duxelles Crostini

Ingredients:

For the mushroom duxelles:

- 8 ounces (about 225g) mushrooms (such as button mushrooms or cremini mushrooms), cleaned and finely chopped
- 2 tablespoons unsalted butter
- 1 small shallot, finely chopped
- 2 cloves garlic, minced
- 1 tablespoon chopped fresh thyme leaves
- Salt and freshly ground black pepper, to taste
- 2 tablespoons dry white wine (optional)
- 2 tablespoons heavy cream (optional)

For the crostini:

- 1 baguette, sliced into 1/2-inch thick rounds
- 2 tablespoons olive oil
- Salt and freshly ground black pepper, to taste
- Grated Parmesan cheese, for garnish (optional)
- Fresh parsley, chopped, for garnish (optional)

Instructions:

1. Preheat your oven to 375°F (190°C). Line a baking sheet with parchment paper.
2. Arrange the baguette slices on the prepared baking sheet. Brush both sides of each slice with olive oil and sprinkle with salt and pepper.
3. Bake the baguette slices in the preheated oven for 10-12 minutes, or until golden brown and crispy. Remove from the oven and let cool slightly.
4. Meanwhile, prepare the mushroom duxelles. In a large skillet, melt the butter over medium heat. Add the finely chopped shallot and garlic, and cook until softened and fragrant, about 2-3 minutes.

5. Add the chopped mushrooms to the skillet and cook, stirring occasionally, until they release their moisture and start to brown, about 8-10 minutes.
6. Stir in the chopped fresh thyme leaves and season with salt and pepper to taste.
7. If using, deglaze the skillet with dry white wine, scraping up any browned bits from the bottom of the pan. Cook for an additional 2-3 minutes, or until the wine has evaporated.
8. Optionally, stir in the heavy cream to add richness to the mushroom mixture. Cook for another minute, then remove the skillet from the heat.
9. To assemble the crostini, spoon a generous amount of mushroom duxelles onto each toasted baguette slice.
10. If desired, sprinkle grated Parmesan cheese over the top of the mushroom duxelles.
11. Garnish the crostini with chopped fresh parsley for a pop of color and freshness.
12. Serve the mushroom duxelles crostini warm or at room temperature as a delicious appetizer or snack.

Enjoy these flavorful and elegant mushroom duxelles crostini, perfect for entertaining or as a special treat for any occasion!

Salade Niçoise Skewers

Ingredients:

- 12 cherry tomatoes
- 12 small new potatoes, boiled until tender and halved
- 12 green beans, blanched until crisp-tender
- 2 (5-ounce) cans of tuna, drained and flaked
- 12 pitted Kalamata olives
- 4 hard-boiled eggs, peeled and quartered
- 12 small wedges of cooked or steamed artichoke hearts (optional)
- 12 small skewers or toothpicks
- Salt and freshly ground black pepper, to taste
- Extra virgin olive oil, for drizzling
- Lemon wedges, for serving
- Fresh parsley or basil leaves, for garnish (optional)

Instructions:

1. Prepare all the ingredients for assembling the skewers: halve the cherry tomatoes, quarter the hard-boiled eggs, halve the boiled new potatoes, blanch the green beans until crisp-tender, drain and flake the tuna, and drain the olives.
2. Thread the ingredients onto the skewers in any order you prefer, alternating between the cherry tomatoes, new potato halves, green beans, flaked tuna, olives, and hard-boiled egg quarters. Optionally, add a wedge of cooked or steamed artichoke heart between the other ingredients.
3. Season the skewers with salt and freshly ground black pepper to taste.
4. Arrange the Salade Niçoise skewers on a serving platter.
5. Just before serving, drizzle the skewers lightly with extra virgin olive oil.
6. Garnish the skewers with fresh parsley or basil leaves, if desired.
7. Serve the Salade Niçoise skewers with lemon wedges on the side for squeezing over the top.

These Salade Niçoise skewers make a delightful and colorful appetizer or light meal, perfect for serving at parties, picnics, or any occasion where you want to impress your guests with a taste of French cuisine!

Brandade de Morue (Salt Cod Spread)

Ingredients:

- 1 lb (about 450g) salt cod (bacalao), soaked overnight in cold water
- 1 lb (about 450g) russet potatoes, peeled and diced
- 4 cloves garlic, peeled
- 1/2 cup (120ml) extra virgin olive oil
- 1/4 cup (60ml) milk or heavy cream (optional)
- Salt and freshly ground black pepper, to taste
- Chopped fresh parsley, for garnish (optional)
- Toasted bread or crackers, for serving

Instructions:

1. Drain the soaked salt cod and rinse it under cold water. Place the cod in a large pot and cover it with fresh cold water. Bring the water to a gentle simmer over medium heat and cook the cod for about 10-15 minutes, or until it flakes easily with a fork.
2. While the cod is cooking, place the diced potatoes and garlic cloves in a separate pot and cover them with cold water. Bring the water to a boil, then reduce the heat to medium and cook the potatoes and garlic until they are tender, about 10-15 minutes.
3. Drain the cooked cod, potatoes, and garlic, and transfer them to a large mixing bowl. Mash the mixture with a potato masher or fork until smooth and well combined.
4. Gradually add the olive oil to the cod and potato mixture, stirring continuously, until the mixture is creamy and emulsified. If desired, stir in the milk or heavy cream to achieve a smoother consistency.
5. Season the Brandade de Morue with salt and freshly ground black pepper to taste. Adjust the seasoning if needed.
6. Transfer the Brandade de Morue to a serving dish and garnish with chopped fresh parsley, if desired.
7. Serve the Brandade de Morue warm or at room temperature, accompanied by toasted bread or crackers for spreading.

Enjoy this delicious and comforting Brandade de Morue as a flavorful appetizer or snack, perfect for sharing with family and friends!

Tarte Flambée (Alsatian Pizza)

Ingredients:

For the dough:

- 1 1/2 cups (180g) all-purpose flour
- 1/2 teaspoon salt
- 1/2 teaspoon sugar
- 1/2 teaspoon instant yeast
- 1/2 cup (120ml) warm water
- 1 tablespoon olive oil

For the topping:

- 1/2 cup (120g) crème fraîche or fromage blanc
- 1 large onion, thinly sliced
- 4 ounces (about 115g) lardons or thick-cut bacon, diced
- Salt and freshly ground black pepper, to taste
- Fresh thyme leaves or chopped parsley, for garnish (optional)

Instructions:

1. In a large mixing bowl, combine the flour, salt, sugar, and instant yeast. Gradually add the warm water and olive oil, stirring until a dough forms.
2. Turn the dough out onto a lightly floured surface and knead it for about 5-7 minutes, or until smooth and elastic. Shape the dough into a ball.
3. Place the dough in a lightly oiled bowl, cover it with a clean kitchen towel or plastic wrap, and let it rise in a warm, draft-free place for about 1 hour, or until doubled in size.
4. While the dough is rising, prepare the topping. In a skillet, cook the diced bacon or lardons over medium heat until crispy. Remove the cooked bacon from the skillet and set aside, leaving the rendered fat in the pan.
5. Add the thinly sliced onions to the skillet with the rendered bacon fat and cook over medium-low heat, stirring occasionally, until the onions are soft and caramelized, about 15-20 minutes. Season with salt and pepper to taste. Remove from heat and let cool slightly.

6. Preheat your oven to 475°F (245°C). If using a pizza stone, place it in the oven to preheat as well.
7. Once the dough has risen, punch it down and divide it into two equal portions. Roll out each portion of dough on a lightly floured surface into a thin rectangle or oval shape, about 1/8 inch thick.
8. Transfer the rolled-out dough to a parchment paper-lined baking sheet or a pizza peel dusted with cornmeal, if using a pizza stone.
9. Spread a thin layer of crème fraîche or fromage blanc over each portion of dough, leaving a small border around the edges.
10. Divide the caramelized onions and cooked bacon/lardons evenly between the two tarte flambées, spreading them out in an even layer over the crème fraîche.
11. Transfer the tarte flambées to the preheated oven (or onto the preheated pizza stone) and bake for 10-12 minutes, or until the crust is golden brown and crispy and the toppings are bubbly and lightly browned.
12. Remove from the oven and let cool slightly before slicing.
13. Garnish with fresh thyme leaves or chopped parsley, if desired, before serving.

Enjoy this classic Alsatian dish, Tarte Flambée, as a delicious appetizer or main course, perfect for sharing with family and friends!

Brie and Pear Tartlets

Ingredients:

- 1 sheet of puff pastry, thawed if frozen
- 1 ripe pear, thinly sliced
- 4 ounces (about 115g) Brie cheese, rind removed and cut into small cubes
- 2 tablespoons honey
- Fresh thyme leaves, for garnish (optional)

Instructions:

1. Preheat your oven to 375°F (190°C). Line a baking sheet with parchment paper or a silicone baking mat.
2. Roll out the puff pastry sheet on a lightly floured surface to about 1/8 inch thickness. Use a round cookie cutter or a sharp knife to cut out circles from the puff pastry, each about 3-4 inches in diameter.
3. Transfer the puff pastry circles to the prepared baking sheet.
4. Place a few cubes of Brie cheese in the center of each puff pastry circle.
5. Top the Brie cheese with a slice of pear.
6. Drizzle each tartlet with a little honey.
7. Bake in the preheated oven for 15-18 minutes, or until the puff pastry is golden brown and puffed up, and the Brie cheese is melted and bubbly.
8. Remove from the oven and let the tartlets cool slightly on the baking sheet.
9. Garnish each tartlet with fresh thyme leaves, if desired, before serving.
10. Serve the Brie and pear tartlets warm as a delicious appetizer or snack.

These Brie and pear tartlets are sure to impress with their combination of sweet and savory flavors and their elegant presentation. Enjoy them for any occasion, from casual gatherings to special celebrations!

Foie Gras Mousse with Fig Jam

Ingredients:

For the foie gras mousse:

- 8 ounces (about 225g) foie gras, chilled
- 1/4 cup (60ml) heavy cream
- 1 tablespoon cognac or brandy
- 1/4 teaspoon salt
- 1/8 teaspoon freshly ground black pepper

For the fig jam:

- 8 ounces (about 225g) fresh figs, stemmed and chopped
- 1/4 cup (60ml) water
- 2 tablespoons honey or sugar
- 1 tablespoon lemon juice
- Pinch of salt

For serving:

- Crostini or toasted baguette slices

Instructions:

1. Prepare the foie gras mousse:
    - Cut the chilled foie gras into small pieces and place them in a food processor.
    - Add the heavy cream, cognac or brandy, salt, and black pepper to the food processor.
    - Process the mixture until smooth and creamy, scraping down the sides of the bowl as needed. The consistency should be similar to a mousse.

- Transfer the foie gras mousse to a bowl, cover with plastic wrap, and refrigerate for at least 1 hour to chill and firm up.
2. Prepare the fig jam:
    - In a small saucepan, combine the chopped figs, water, honey or sugar, lemon juice, and a pinch of salt.
    - Bring the mixture to a simmer over medium heat, then reduce the heat to low and let it cook, stirring occasionally, for about 20-25 minutes, or until the figs are soft and the mixture has thickened to a jam-like consistency.
    - Remove the saucepan from the heat and let the fig jam cool slightly.
3. Assemble the foie gras mousse with fig jam:
    - Once the foie gras mousse is chilled and firm, remove it from the refrigerator.
    - Spoon a dollop of foie gras mousse onto each crostini or toasted baguette slice.
    - Top each crostini with a spoonful of fig jam, spreading it gently over the mousse.
4. Serve the foie gras mousse with fig jam immediately as a luxurious appetizer.

Enjoy the decadent combination of creamy foie gras mousse and sweet fig jam on crispy crostini, perfect for special occasions or elegant gatherings!

Stuffed Mushrooms with Boursin Cheese

Ingredients:

- 16 large button or cremini mushrooms, stems removed and reserved
- 1 tablespoon olive oil
- 2 cloves garlic, minced
- 1/4 cup finely chopped onion
- 4 ounces (about 115g) Boursin cheese, softened
- 2 tablespoons grated Parmesan cheese
- 1 tablespoon chopped fresh parsley
- Salt and freshly ground black pepper, to taste
- Bread crumbs, for topping (optional)
- Fresh parsley leaves, for garnish (optional)

Instructions:

1. Preheat your oven to 375°F (190°C). Line a baking sheet with parchment paper or aluminum foil.
2. Clean the mushrooms with a damp paper towel to remove any dirt. Carefully remove the stems from the mushrooms and finely chop them. Set aside.
3. In a skillet, heat the olive oil over medium heat. Add the minced garlic and chopped onion, and sauté until softened and fragrant, about 2-3 minutes. Add the chopped mushroom stems and cook for another 3-4 minutes, until they release their moisture and become tender. Remove from heat and let cool slightly.
4. In a mixing bowl, combine the softened Boursin cheese, grated Parmesan cheese, chopped parsley, and the sautéed mushroom mixture. Season with salt and pepper to taste, and mix until well combined.
5. Spoon the Boursin cheese mixture into the cavity of each mushroom cap, filling them generously.
6. If desired, sprinkle bread crumbs over the top of each stuffed mushroom for added texture.
7. Place the stuffed mushrooms on the prepared baking sheet and bake in the preheated oven for 15-20 minutes, or until the mushrooms are tender and the filling is golden brown and bubbly.
8. Remove from the oven and let the stuffed mushrooms cool slightly before serving.

9. Garnish with fresh parsley leaves, if desired, before serving.

These stuffed mushrooms with Boursin cheese are sure to impress your guests with their creamy and flavorful filling. Enjoy them warm as a delicious appetizer or snack!

Potato Leek Soup Shooters

Ingredients:

- 2 leeks, white and light green parts only, thinly sliced
- 2 tablespoons unsalted butter
- 2 cloves garlic, minced
- 1 lb (about 450g) potatoes, peeled and diced
- 4 cups (960ml) chicken or vegetable broth
- 1/2 cup (120ml) heavy cream
- Salt and freshly ground black pepper, to taste
- Chopped fresh chives or parsley, for garnish (optional)

Instructions:

1. In a large pot or Dutch oven, melt the butter over medium heat. Add the sliced leeks and minced garlic, and cook until softened, about 5-7 minutes.
2. Add the diced potatoes to the pot and stir to combine with the leeks and garlic.
3. Pour in the chicken or vegetable broth, making sure the potatoes are covered. Bring the mixture to a boil, then reduce the heat to low and simmer, covered, for about 15-20 minutes, or until the potatoes are tender and cooked through.
4. Using an immersion blender or regular blender, blend the soup until smooth and creamy. If using a regular blender, work in batches and be careful when blending hot liquids.
5. Stir in the heavy cream and season the soup with salt and pepper to taste. Adjust the seasoning if needed.
6. If the soup is too thick, you can thin it out with a little more broth or water until you reach your desired consistency.
7. Once the soup is ready, ladle it into shot glasses or small cups.
8. Garnish each potato leek soup shooter with chopped fresh chives or parsley, if desired.
9. Serve the potato leek soup shooters immediately as a delicious appetizer or starter.

These potato leek soup shooters are sure to impress your guests with their creamy texture and comforting flavor. Enjoy them warm as a delightful addition to any gathering!

Smoked Salmon Canapés

Ingredients:

- Thinly sliced smoked salmon
- Baguette or crackers, thinly sliced
- Cream cheese or goat cheese, softened
- Cucumber, thinly sliced
- Red onion, thinly sliced
- Capers
- Fresh dill or chives, chopped
- Lemon wedges, for serving

Instructions:

1. Slice the baguette into thin rounds or cut the crackers into bite-sized pieces.
2. Spread a thin layer of cream cheese or goat cheese onto each slice of baguette or cracker.
3. Top each slice with a slice of smoked salmon, folding or arranging it neatly on top of the cheese.
4. Place a slice of cucumber on top of the smoked salmon.
5. Add a few thin slices of red onion on top of the cucumber.
6. Garnish each canapé with a few capers and a sprinkle of chopped fresh dill or chives.
7. Arrange the smoked salmon canapés on a serving platter.
8. Serve the canapés immediately, with lemon wedges on the side for squeezing over the top, if desired.

These smoked salmon canapés are sure to impress your guests with their beautiful presentation and delicious flavors. Enjoy them as an elegant appetizer or part of a larger spread at your next gathering!

Pâté de Campagne (Country Pâté)

Ingredients:

- 1 lb (about 450g) ground pork
- 8 oz (about 225g) pork liver, finely chopped
- 4 slices bacon, chopped
- 1 small onion, finely chopped
- 2 cloves garlic, minced
- 1/4 cup (60ml) dry white wine
- 2 tablespoons brandy or cognac
- 1 teaspoon dried thyme
- 1/2 teaspoon dried sage
- 1/2 teaspoon dried marjoram
- 1/4 teaspoon ground allspice
- 1/4 teaspoon ground nutmeg
- Salt and freshly ground black pepper, to taste
- 1/2 cup (120ml) heavy cream
- 1/2 cup (60g) breadcrumbs
- 2 eggs
- 3 tablespoons chopped fresh parsley
- Butter, for greasing the terrine mold

Instructions:

1. Preheat your oven to 350°F (175°C). Grease a terrine mold or loaf pan with butter.
2. In a large skillet, cook the chopped bacon over medium heat until crispy. Remove the bacon from the skillet and set aside, leaving the rendered fat in the pan.
3. Add the finely chopped onion to the skillet and cook until softened, about 5 minutes. Add the minced garlic and cook for another minute.
4. Add the ground pork and chopped pork liver to the skillet, breaking up any clumps with a spoon. Cook until the meat is browned and cooked through.
5. Deglaze the skillet with white wine and brandy, scraping up any browned bits from the bottom of the pan. Cook for a few minutes to reduce the liquid.
6. Stir in the dried thyme, sage, marjoram, allspice, and nutmeg. Season with salt and pepper to taste.

7. In a separate bowl, whisk together the heavy cream, breadcrumbs, and eggs until well combined.
8. Add the breadcrumb mixture to the skillet with the cooked meat and stir until evenly combined. Stir in the chopped fresh parsley and cooked bacon.
9. Transfer the mixture to the greased terrine mold or loaf pan, pressing it down firmly with a spoon to remove any air pockets.
10. Cover the terrine mold or loaf pan with aluminum foil and place it in a larger baking dish. Fill the baking dish with hot water until it reaches halfway up the sides of the terrine mold or loaf pan.
11. Bake in the preheated oven for 1 1/2 to 2 hours, or until the pâté is firm and cooked through. Remove the foil during the last 30 minutes of baking to allow the top to brown slightly.
12. Once cooked, remove the pâté from the oven and let it cool to room temperature. Refrigerate the pâté for at least 4 hours, or preferably overnight, to allow it to set.
13. To serve, slice the chilled pâté and serve it with crusty bread, mustard, cornichons, and other accompaniments.

Enjoy this homemade Pâté de Campagne as a delicious appetizer or part of a charcuterie board, and impress your guests with its rustic charm and rich flavors!

Caramelized Onion and Bacon Tartlets

Ingredients:

For the pastry crust:

- 1 1/4 cups (155g) all-purpose flour
- 1/2 teaspoon salt
- 1/2 cup (115g) unsalted butter, cold and cut into cubes
- 2-3 tablespoons ice water

For the filling:

- 4 slices bacon, chopped
- 2 large onions, thinly sliced
- 2 tablespoons unsalted butter
- 1 tablespoon olive oil
- 1 teaspoon sugar
- Salt and freshly ground black pepper, to taste
- 1/2 cup (60g) grated Gruyère cheese or Swiss cheese
- Fresh thyme leaves, for garnish (optional)

Instructions:

1. Preheat your oven to 375°F (190°C). Grease a mini muffin tin with butter or non-stick cooking spray.
2. To make the pastry crust, in a food processor, combine the flour and salt. Add the cold cubed butter and pulse until the mixture resembles coarse crumbs.
3. Gradually add the ice water, one tablespoon at a time, and pulse until the dough comes together and forms a ball. Be careful not to overmix.
4. Transfer the dough to a lightly floured surface and roll it out to about 1/8 inch thickness. Use a round cookie cutter or glass to cut out circles slightly larger than the mini muffin tin cavities.
5. Press each dough circle into the cavities of the mini muffin tin, forming small tartlet shells. Prick the bottoms of the shells with a fork to prevent them from puffing up during baking.

6. Bake the tartlet shells in the preheated oven for 10-12 minutes, or until lightly golden brown. Remove from the oven and let cool slightly.
7. While the tartlet shells are baking, prepare the filling. In a skillet, cook the chopped bacon over medium heat until crispy. Remove the bacon from the skillet and drain on paper towels.
8. In the same skillet, add the butter and olive oil. Add the thinly sliced onions and sugar, and cook over medium-low heat, stirring occasionally, until the onions are caramelized and golden brown, about 20-25 minutes. Season with salt and pepper to taste.
9. Once the tartlet shells have cooled slightly, spoon a small amount of caramelized onions into each shell.
10. Top the caramelized onions with a sprinkle of crispy bacon pieces.
11. Sprinkle grated Gruyère or Swiss cheese over the bacon and onions in each tartlet shell.
12. Return the tartlets to the oven and bake for an additional 5-7 minutes, or until the cheese is melted and bubbly.
13. Remove from the oven and let the tartlets cool slightly in the muffin tin before carefully removing them.
14. Garnish each tartlet with fresh thyme leaves, if desired, before serving.

These caramelized onion and bacon tartlets are best served warm as a delicious and savory appetizer, sure to impress your guests with their rich flavors and elegant presentation!

Chicken Liver Pâté with Cornichons

Ingredients:

- 1 lb (about 450g) chicken livers, trimmed and cleaned
- 1 small onion, finely chopped
- 2 cloves garlic, minced
- 4 tablespoons unsalted butter
- 2 tablespoons brandy or cognac
- 1 teaspoon dried thyme
- 1/2 teaspoon dried sage
- 1/4 teaspoon ground allspice
- Salt and freshly ground black pepper, to taste
- 1/2 cup (120ml) heavy cream
- Cornichons, for serving
- Crackers or toasted bread, for serving

Instructions:

1. In a large skillet, melt 2 tablespoons of butter over medium heat. Add the chopped onion and minced garlic, and cook until softened and translucent, about 5 minutes.
2. Add the cleaned chicken livers to the skillet and cook until browned on the outside but still slightly pink on the inside, about 3-4 minutes per side. Be careful not to overcook the livers, as they can become tough.
3. Deglaze the skillet with brandy or cognac, scraping up any browned bits from the bottom of the pan. Cook for another minute to allow the alcohol to evaporate.
4. Stir in the dried thyme, sage, and ground allspice. Season with salt and freshly ground black pepper to taste.
5. Transfer the mixture to a food processor or blender. Add the remaining 2 tablespoons of butter and the heavy cream.
6. Blend the mixture until smooth and creamy, scraping down the sides of the bowl as needed. If the pâté is too thick, you can add more cream or butter to reach your desired consistency.
7. Taste and adjust the seasoning if needed, adding more salt, pepper, or herbs to taste.

8. Transfer the chicken liver pâté to a serving dish or ramekins. Smooth the top with a spatula.
9. Cover the pâté with plastic wrap and refrigerate for at least 2 hours, or until firm and chilled.
10. Serve the chicken liver pâté with cornichons and crackers or toasted bread for spreading.

Enjoy this delicious and indulgent chicken liver pâté with cornichons as a savory appetizer, perfect for entertaining or special occasions!

Provençal Tomato Tart

Ingredients:

For the pastry crust:

- 1 1/4 cups (155g) all-purpose flour
- 1/2 teaspoon salt
- 1/2 cup (115g) unsalted butter, cold and cut into cubes
- 2-3 tablespoons ice water

For the filling:

- 4-5 ripe tomatoes, thinly sliced
- 1 tablespoon Dijon mustard
- 1 cup (100g) grated Gruyère cheese or Swiss cheese
- 2 tablespoons chopped fresh basil
- 2 tablespoons chopped fresh thyme
- 2 tablespoons chopped fresh parsley
- Salt and freshly ground black pepper, to taste
- Olive oil, for drizzling

Instructions:

1. Preheat your oven to 375°F (190°C). Grease a tart pan or pie dish with butter or non-stick cooking spray.
2. To make the pastry crust, in a food processor, combine the flour and salt. Add the cold cubed butter and pulse until the mixture resembles coarse crumbs.
3. Gradually add the ice water, one tablespoon at a time, and pulse until the dough comes together and forms a ball. Be careful not to overmix.
4. Transfer the dough to a lightly floured surface and roll it out to fit the tart pan or pie dish. Press the dough into the bottom and sides of the pan, trimming any excess.

5. Prick the bottom of the crust with a fork to prevent it from puffing up during baking. Blind bake the crust in the preheated oven for about 15 minutes, or until lightly golden brown. Remove from the oven and let cool slightly.
6. While the crust is baking, prepare the filling. Spread the Dijon mustard evenly over the bottom of the partially baked crust.
7. Arrange the thinly sliced tomatoes in an overlapping pattern over the mustard.
8. Sprinkle the grated Gruyère or Swiss cheese over the tomatoes.
9. Scatter the chopped fresh basil, thyme, and parsley over the cheese. Season with salt and freshly ground black pepper to taste.
10. Drizzle a little olive oil over the top of the tart.
11. Return the tart to the oven and bake for an additional 20-25 minutes, or until the tomatoes are tender and the cheese is melted and bubbly.
12. Remove from the oven and let the tart cool slightly before slicing.
13. Serve the Provençal tomato tart warm or at room temperature, garnished with additional fresh herbs if desired.

Enjoy this delicious Provençal tomato tart as a flavorful appetizer or light meal, perfect for showcasing the flavors of summer!

Shrimp Cocktail with Sauce Marie Rose

Ingredients:

For the pastry crust:

- 1 1/4 cups (155g) all-purpose flour
- 1/2 teaspoon salt
- 1/2 cup (115g) unsalted butter, cold and cut into cubes
- 2-3 tablespoons ice water

For the filling:

- 4-5 ripe tomatoes, thinly sliced
- 1 tablespoon Dijon mustard
- 1 cup (100g) grated Gruyère cheese or Swiss cheese
- 2 tablespoons chopped fresh basil
- 2 tablespoons chopped fresh thyme
- 2 tablespoons chopped fresh parsley
- Salt and freshly ground black pepper, to taste
- Olive oil, for drizzling

Instructions:

1. Preheat your oven to 375°F (190°C). Grease a tart pan or pie dish with butter or non-stick cooking spray.
2. To make the pastry crust, in a food processor, combine the flour and salt. Add the cold cubed butter and pulse until the mixture resembles coarse crumbs.
3. Gradually add the ice water, one tablespoon at a time, and pulse until the dough comes together and forms a ball. Be careful not to overmix.
4. Transfer the dough to a lightly floured surface and roll it out to fit the tart pan or pie dish. Press the dough into the bottom and sides of the pan, trimming any excess.

5. Prick the bottom of the crust with a fork to prevent it from puffing up during baking. Blind bake the crust in the preheated oven for about 15 minutes, or until lightly golden brown. Remove from the oven and let cool slightly.
6. While the crust is baking, prepare the filling. Spread the Dijon mustard evenly over the bottom of the partially baked crust.
7. Arrange the thinly sliced tomatoes in an overlapping pattern over the mustard.
8. Sprinkle the grated Gruyère or Swiss cheese over the tomatoes.
9. Scatter the chopped fresh basil, thyme, and parsley over the cheese. Season with salt and freshly ground black pepper to taste.
10. Drizzle a little olive oil over the top of the tart.
11. Return the tart to the oven and bake for an additional 20-25 minutes, or until the tomatoes are tender and the cheese is melted and bubbly.
12. Remove from the oven and let the tart cool slightly before slicing.
13. Serve the Provençal tomato tart warm or at room temperature, garnished with additional fresh herbs if desired.

Enjoy this delicious Provençal tomato tart as a flavorful appetizer or light meal, perfect for showcasing the flavors of summer!

Shrimp Cocktail with Sauce Marie Rose

Shrimp cocktail with sauce Marie Rose is a classic appetizer that combines tender poached shrimp with a creamy and tangy Marie Rose sauce. This dish is elegant and perfect for entertaining. Here's a simple recipe to make shrimp cocktail with sauce Marie Rose at home:

Ingredients:

For the shrimp:

- 1 lb (about 450g) large shrimp, peeled and deveined, tails intact
- 1 lemon, halved
- 2 bay leaves
- 1 teaspoon whole peppercorns
- Salt, to taste
- Ice water, for chilling

For the sauce Marie Rose:

- 1/2 cup (120g) mayonnaise
- 2 tablespoons ketchup
- 1 tablespoon lemon juice
- 1 teaspoon Worcestershire sauce
- Tabasco sauce, to taste (optional)
- Salt and freshly ground black pepper, to taste

For serving:

- Lettuce leaves
- Lemon wedges, for garnish
- Chopped fresh parsley or dill, for garnish (optional)

Instructions:

1. Bring a large pot of water to a boil. Squeeze the lemon halves into the boiling water and add the lemon halves, bay leaves, peppercorns, and salt.
2. Add the shrimp to the boiling water and cook for 2-3 minutes, or until they turn pink and opaque. Be careful not to overcook the shrimp.
3. Drain the shrimp and immediately transfer them to a bowl of ice water to stop the cooking process and chill them quickly. Once chilled, drain the shrimp and pat them dry with paper towels.
4. In a small bowl, whisk together the mayonnaise, ketchup, lemon juice, Worcestershire sauce, and Tabasco sauce (if using) until well combined. Season with salt and freshly ground black pepper to taste. Adjust the seasoning and spiciness according to your preference.
5. Arrange the lettuce leaves on a serving platter or individual plates.
6. Place the chilled shrimp on top of the lettuce leaves.
7. Spoon the sauce Marie Rose over the shrimp, covering them evenly.
8. Garnish with lemon wedges and chopped fresh parsley or dill, if desired.
9. Serve the shrimp cocktail immediately, with additional sauce Marie Rose on the side.

Enjoy this classic shrimp cocktail with sauce Marie Rose as a refreshing and flavorful appetizer, perfect for any occasion!

Mushroom and Gruyère Tartlets

Ingredients:

For the pastry crust:

- 1 1/4 cups (155g) all-purpose flour
- 1/2 teaspoon salt
- 1/2 cup (115g) unsalted butter, cold and cut into cubes
- 2-3 tablespoons ice water

For the filling:

- 2 tablespoons unsalted butter
- 8 ounces (about 225g) mushrooms (such as cremini or button), thinly sliced
- 1 small shallot, finely chopped
- 2 cloves garlic, minced
- Salt and freshly ground black pepper, to taste
- 1/2 cup (120ml) heavy cream
- 1 cup (100g) grated Gruyère cheese
- Fresh thyme leaves, for garnish (optional)

Instructions:

1. Preheat your oven to 375°F (190°C). Grease a mini muffin tin with butter or non-stick cooking spray.
2. To make the pastry crust, in a food processor, combine the flour and salt. Add the cold cubed butter and pulse until the mixture resembles coarse crumbs.
3. Gradually add the ice water, one tablespoon at a time, and pulse until the dough comes together and forms a ball. Be careful not to overmix.
4. Transfer the dough to a lightly floured surface and roll it out to about 1/8 inch thickness. Use a round cookie cutter or glass to cut out circles slightly larger than the mini muffin tin cavities.

5. Press each dough circle into the cavities of the mini muffin tin, forming small tartlet shells. Prick the bottoms of the shells with a fork to prevent them from puffing up during baking.
6. Bake the tartlet shells in the preheated oven for 10-12 minutes, or until lightly golden brown. Remove from the oven and let cool slightly.
7. While the tartlet shells are baking, prepare the filling. In a skillet, melt the butter over medium heat. Add the sliced mushrooms, chopped shallot, and minced garlic. Cook, stirring occasionally, until the mushrooms are softened and any liquid has evaporated, about 8-10 minutes. Season with salt and freshly ground black pepper to taste.
8. Stir in the heavy cream and cook for another 2-3 minutes, until the cream has thickened slightly.
9. Remove the skillet from the heat and stir in the grated Gruyère cheese until melted and combined with the mushroom mixture.
10. Spoon the mushroom and Gruyère filling into the baked tartlet shells, filling each one almost to the top.
11. Return the tartlets to the oven and bake for an additional 5-7 minutes, or until the filling is bubbly and lightly golden brown on top.
12. Remove from the oven and let the tartlets cool slightly in the muffin tin before carefully removing them.
13. Garnish each tartlet with fresh thyme leaves, if desired, before serving.

These mushroom and Gruyère tartlets are best served warm as a delicious and savory appetizer, perfect for entertaining or special occasions!

Crab Stuffed Mushrooms

Ingredients:

- 12 large mushrooms, cleaned with stems removed
- 8 ounces (225g) lump crabmeat, drained and picked over for shells
- 4 ounces (115g) cream cheese, softened
- 1/4 cup (60ml) mayonnaise
- 1/4 cup (25g) grated Parmesan cheese
- 2 green onions, finely chopped
- 1 clove garlic, minced
- 1 teaspoon Worcestershire sauce
- 1/2 teaspoon Old Bay seasoning (or to taste)
- Salt and pepper, to taste
- 2 tablespoons breadcrumbs (optional)
- Fresh parsley, chopped, for garnish

Instructions:

1. Preheat your oven to 375°F (190°C). Grease a baking dish with butter or cooking spray.
2. In a mixing bowl, combine the cream cheese, mayonnaise, Parmesan cheese, green onions, garlic, Worcestershire sauce, Old Bay seasoning, salt, and pepper. Mix until well combined.
3. Gently fold in the lump crabmeat until evenly distributed throughout the mixture.
4. Spoon the crab mixture into each mushroom cap, filling them generously and mounding the filling on top.
5. If desired, sprinkle breadcrumbs over the top of each stuffed mushroom for added texture.
6. Arrange the stuffed mushrooms in the prepared baking dish.
7. Bake in the preheated oven for 18-20 minutes, or until the mushrooms are tender and the filling is heated through and lightly golden on top.
8. Remove from the oven and let the stuffed mushrooms cool slightly before serving.
9. Garnish with chopped fresh parsley before serving.

These crab stuffed mushrooms are perfect for parties, gatherings, or as a special appetizer for a dinner party. Enjoy the delicious combination of tender mushrooms and flavorful crab filling!

Fougasse (French Flatbread)

Ingredients:

- 3 cups (375g) all-purpose flour
- 1 teaspoon salt
- 1 teaspoon sugar
- 1 packet (2 1/4 teaspoons) active dry yeast
- 1 cup (240ml) warm water (about 110°F or 45°C)
- 3 tablespoons olive oil
- Optional toppings: chopped olives, herbs (such as rosemary or thyme), grated cheese (such as Parmesan or Gruyère), sea salt flakes

Instructions:

1. In a large mixing bowl, combine the flour, salt, and sugar. Make a well in the center.
2. In a small bowl, mix the warm water and yeast together. Let it sit for about 5 minutes until foamy.
3. Pour the yeast mixture into the well of the dry ingredients. Add the olive oil.
4. Stir the mixture with a wooden spoon until a dough starts to form.
5. Turn the dough out onto a floured surface and knead for about 5-7 minutes until the dough is smooth and elastic.
6. Place the dough in a lightly oiled bowl, cover with a clean kitchen towel, and let it rise in a warm place for about 1 hour, or until doubled in size.
7. Preheat your oven to 400°F (200°C). Line a baking sheet with parchment paper.
8. Punch down the risen dough and turn it out onto a floured surface. Divide the dough into two equal portions.
9. Roll out each portion of dough into a rough oval or rectangular shape, about 1/4 inch (0.5cm) thick.
10. Use a sharp knife or pizza cutter to make several diagonal slashes across the surface of the dough to create a leaf or ear shape. Be careful not to cut all the way through the dough.
11. If desired, sprinkle the dough with your choice of toppings such as chopped olives, herbs, cheese, or sea salt flakes.
12. Transfer the shaped dough onto the prepared baking sheet.
13. Bake in the preheated oven for 15-20 minutes, or until the fougasse is golden brown and cooked through.

14. Remove from the oven and let the fougasse cool slightly on a wire rack before serving.

Fougasse is best served warm and can be enjoyed on its own or alongside soups, salads, or charcuterie boards. Enjoy the delicious flavors of this French flatbread!

Duck Rillettes

Ingredients:

- 2 lbs (about 900g) duck legs or duck leg quarters
- 2 cloves garlic, minced
- 2 shallots, finely chopped
- 2 sprigs fresh thyme
- 2 bay leaves
- Salt and freshly ground black pepper, to taste
- 1/2 cup (120ml) dry white wine
- Duck fat (or substitute rendered duck fat, chicken fat, or pork fat)
- Toasted bread or crackers, for serving
- Cornichons and mustard, for serving (optional)

Instructions:

1. Preheat your oven to 300°F (150°C).
2. Season the duck legs generously with salt and pepper on both sides.
3. In a large oven-safe Dutch oven or heavy-bottomed pot, heat a small amount of duck fat over medium-high heat. Add the duck legs to the pot, skin side down, and sear until golden brown, about 5-7 minutes. Flip the duck legs and sear the other side for an additional 5 minutes. Remove the duck legs from the pot and set aside.
4. Add the minced garlic and chopped shallots to the pot and cook until softened and fragrant, about 2-3 minutes.
5. Return the duck legs to the pot, along with the fresh thyme sprigs, bay leaves, and white wine. Bring the mixture to a simmer.
6. Cover the pot with a tight-fitting lid and transfer it to the preheated oven. Cook for 2-3 hours, or until the duck meat is very tender and falling off the bone.
7. Remove the pot from the oven and let the duck legs cool slightly. Remove the skin and bones from the duck legs, and shred the meat using two forks or your fingers. Discard the skin and bones.
8. Transfer the shredded duck meat to a mixing bowl and season with additional salt and pepper to taste. You can also add a splash of the cooking liquid from the pot to moisten the meat, if desired.

9. Pack the shredded duck meat tightly into small jars or ramekins, pressing down firmly to remove any air pockets.
10. Melt the duck fat in a saucepan over low heat until it is completely liquid. Pour the melted duck fat over the top of the shredded duck meat in each jar or ramekin, making sure the meat is completely submerged.
11. Let the duck rillettes cool to room temperature, then cover with lids or plastic wrap and refrigerate for at least 4 hours, or preferably overnight, to allow the flavors to meld and the duck fat to solidify.
12. Serve the duck rillettes chilled or at room temperature, spread on toasted bread or crackers. Garnish with cornichons and mustard, if desired.

Enjoy this delicious and flavorful duck rillettes as a sophisticated appetizer or part of a charcuterie board, and impress your guests with its rich taste and creamy texture!

Goat Cheese and Herb Stuffed Cherry Tomatoes

Ingredients:

- 24 cherry tomatoes
- 4 ounces (about 115g) goat cheese, softened
- 2 tablespoons chopped fresh herbs (such as basil, parsley, chives, or thyme)
- 1 tablespoon extra-virgin olive oil
- 1 clove garlic, minced
- Salt and freshly ground black pepper, to taste
- Fresh basil leaves, for garnish (optional)

Instructions:

1. Slice the top off each cherry tomato and carefully scoop out the seeds and pulp using a small spoon or melon baller. Discard the seeds and pulp, or reserve them for another use.
2. In a mixing bowl, combine the softened goat cheese, chopped fresh herbs, minced garlic, and extra-virgin olive oil. Mix until well combined.
3. Season the goat cheese mixture with salt and freshly ground black pepper to taste. Adjust the seasoning according to your preference.
4. Using a small spoon or piping bag fitted with a small round tip, fill each hollowed-out cherry tomato with the goat cheese mixture, mounding it slightly on top.
5. Arrange the stuffed cherry tomatoes on a serving platter or plate.
6. If desired, garnish each stuffed cherry tomato with a small fresh basil leaf for added flavor and presentation.
7. Serve the goat cheese and herb stuffed cherry tomatoes immediately, or refrigerate them for up to an hour before serving to allow the flavors to meld.

These goat cheese and herb stuffed cherry tomatoes are sure to impress your guests with their vibrant colors and delicious flavors. Enjoy them as a tasty and elegant appetizer for any occasion!

Tartine with Tapenade and Anchovies

Ingredients:

- 4 slices of crusty bread (such as baguette or ciabatta), toasted
- 1/2 cup (120g) black olive tapenade (homemade or store-bought)
- 8 anchovy fillets, drained (optional)
- Fresh parsley, chopped, for garnish (optional)
- Extra-virgin olive oil, for drizzling (optional)

Instructions:

1. Toast the slices of crusty bread until golden brown and crispy. You can toast them in a toaster, under the broiler, or on a grill.
2. Spread a generous layer of black olive tapenade onto each toasted slice of bread. Use the back of a spoon to spread it evenly.
3. If using anchovy fillets, place two anchovy fillets diagonally on top of each tartine, crossing them over each other.
4. Sprinkle the chopped fresh parsley over the top of the tartines for added flavor and color.
5. Drizzle a little extra-virgin olive oil over the top of the tartines, if desired, for extra richness and flavor.
6. Serve the tartines with tapenade and anchovies immediately, while the bread is still warm and crispy.

These tartines with tapenade and anchovies are perfect as an appetizer or light snack, and they pair wonderfully with a glass of wine or a refreshing cocktail. Enjoy the bold and savory flavors of this classic French dish!

Pork Rillettes

Ingredients:

- 2 lbs (about 900g) boneless pork shoulder, trimmed of excess fat and cut into chunks
- 1/2 lb (about 225g) pork belly, trimmed of excess fat and cut into chunks
- 2 cloves garlic, minced
- 2 shallots, finely chopped
- 2 sprigs fresh thyme
- 2 bay leaves
- Salt and freshly ground black pepper, to taste
- 1/2 cup (120ml) dry white wine
- Pork fat or lard (or substitute rendered duck fat or chicken fat)
- Toasted bread or crackers, for serving

Instructions:

1. Preheat your oven to 300°F (150°C).
2. Season the pork shoulder and pork belly chunks generously with salt and pepper.
3. In a large oven-safe Dutch oven or heavy-bottomed pot, heat a small amount of pork fat or lard over medium-high heat. Add the pork shoulder and pork belly chunks to the pot, in batches if necessary, and sear until golden brown on all sides. Remove the browned pork pieces from the pot and set aside.
4. Add the minced garlic and chopped shallots to the pot and cook until softened and fragrant, about 2-3 minutes.
5. Return the browned pork pieces to the pot, along with the fresh thyme sprigs, bay leaves, and white wine. Bring the mixture to a simmer.
6. Cover the pot with a tight-fitting lid and transfer it to the preheated oven. Cook for 3-4 hours, or until the pork is very tender and falling apart.
7. Remove the pot from the oven and let the pork cool slightly.
8. Using a slotted spoon, transfer the cooked pork pieces to a large mixing bowl. Discard the thyme sprigs and bay leaves.
9. Use two forks or your fingers to shred the pork into small pieces. The meat should be very tender and easily shred apart.
10. Pack the shredded pork tightly into small jars or ramekins, pressing down firmly to remove any air pockets.

11. Melt the pork fat or lard in a saucepan over low heat until it is completely liquid. Pour the melted fat over the top of the shredded pork in each jar or ramekin, making sure the meat is completely covered.
12. Let the pork rillettes cool to room temperature, then cover with lids or plastic wrap and refrigerate for at least 4 hours, or preferably overnight, to allow the flavors to meld and the fat to solidify.
13. Serve the pork rillettes chilled or at room temperature, spread on toasted bread or crackers.

Enjoy these delicious pork rillettes as a flavorful appetizer or part of a charcuterie board, and savor the rich and savory taste of this classic French dish!

Scallop and Bacon Skewers

Ingredients:

- 12 large sea scallops, cleaned and deveined
- 6 slices of bacon, cut in half crosswise
- 1 tablespoon olive oil
- Salt and freshly ground black pepper, to taste
- Lemon wedges, for serving (optional)
- Fresh parsley, chopped, for garnish (optional)

Instructions:

1. Preheat your grill or grill pan to medium-high heat.
2. Pat the scallops dry with paper towels and season them lightly with salt and pepper.
3. Wrap each scallop with a half slice of bacon, securing it with a toothpick or small skewer.
4. Brush the scallops lightly with olive oil to prevent sticking to the grill.
5. Thread the scallops onto metal skewers or soaked wooden skewers, alternating with pieces of bacon.
6. Place the skewers on the preheated grill or grill pan and cook for 3-4 minutes per side, or until the bacon is crispy and the scallops are opaque and slightly firm to the touch.
7. Remove the skewers from the grill and transfer them to a serving platter.
8. Garnish the scallop and bacon skewers with chopped fresh parsley, if desired, and serve immediately with lemon wedges on the side for squeezing over the top.

These scallop and bacon skewers are perfect for serving as an appetizer at parties or as a main course paired with a side salad or vegetables. Enjoy the delicious combination of flavors and textures in this simple yet elegant dish!

Mini Croque-Madame

Ingredients:

- 8 slices of bread (white or whole wheat)
- 4 slices of cooked ham
- 4 slices of Swiss cheese
- 4 teaspoons Dijon mustard
- 4 large eggs
- 2 tablespoons butter
- Salt and pepper, to taste
- Chopped parsley, for garnish (optional)

Instructions:

1. Preheat your oven to 375°F (190°C). Lightly grease a baking sheet or line it with parchment paper.
2. Lay out the slices of bread on a flat surface. Spread 1 teaspoon of Dijon mustard on each slice of bread.
3. Top each slice of bread with a slice of ham and a slice of Swiss cheese.
4. Place another slice of bread on top of each sandwich to form a sandwich.
5. Using a round cookie cutter or a sharp knife, cut out circles from each sandwich. You should get 2 circles per sandwich.
6. In a large skillet, melt the butter over medium heat. Working in batches if necessary, place the mini sandwiches in the skillet and cook until golden brown on both sides, about 2-3 minutes per side. Remove from the skillet and place them on the prepared baking sheet.
7. Once all the mini sandwiches are browned, crack an egg into the center of each sandwich on the baking sheet. Season with salt and pepper.
8. Bake in the preheated oven for 8-10 minutes, or until the egg whites are set and the yolks are still slightly runny.
9. Remove from the oven and garnish with chopped parsley, if desired.
10. Serve the mini Croque-Madame sandwiches immediately, while still warm.

These mini Croque-Madame sandwiches are perfect for brunch, lunch, or as a fun appetizer for parties. Enjoy the delicious combination of flavors and textures in this classic French dish!

Endive Spears with Blue Cheese and Walnuts

Ingredients:

- 2-3 heads of endive
- 4 ounces (about 115g) blue cheese, crumbled
- 1/4 cup (30g) chopped walnuts
- 2 tablespoons honey
- Freshly ground black pepper, to taste
- Fresh parsley or chives, chopped, for garnish (optional)

Instructions:

1. Rinse the endive heads under cold water and pat them dry with paper towels. Trim off the bottom inch of each endive and carefully separate the leaves to create spears. Arrange the endive spears on a serving platter or tray.
2. In a small bowl, combine the crumbled blue cheese and chopped walnuts.
3. Spoon a small amount of the blue cheese and walnut mixture onto each endive spear.
4. Drizzle honey over the top of each endive spear, using more or less depending on your taste preferences.
5. Sprinkle freshly ground black pepper over the top of each endive spear, to taste.
6. If desired, garnish the endive spears with chopped fresh parsley or chives for added color and flavor.
7. Serve the endive spears with blue cheese and walnuts immediately, or refrigerate them for up to 1 hour before serving to allow the flavors to meld.

These endive spears with blue cheese and walnuts are a delicious and elegant appetizer that is sure to impress your guests. Enjoy the delightful combination of flavors and textures in this simple yet sophisticated dish!

Tarte Tatin Bites (Upside-Down Apple Tart)

Ingredients:

- 2-3 large apples (such as Granny Smith or Gala)
- 1/4 cup (50g) granulated sugar
- 2 tablespoons unsalted butter
- 1 sheet puff pastry, thawed if frozen
- Whipped cream or vanilla ice cream, for serving (optional)
- Cinnamon or powdered sugar, for dusting (optional)

Instructions:

1. Preheat your oven to 375°F (190°C). Lightly grease a mini muffin tin with butter or cooking spray.
2. Peel, core, and thinly slice the apples.
3. In a skillet or saucepan, melt the butter over medium heat. Add the granulated sugar and stir until the sugar is dissolved and begins to caramelize, about 3-5 minutes.
4. Add the sliced apples to the caramelized sugar and cook until they are tender and caramelized, about 5-7 minutes. Stir occasionally to ensure even cooking. Remove from heat and let cool slightly.
5. While the apples are cooling, roll out the puff pastry on a lightly floured surface to about 1/8 inch (3mm) thickness. Use a round cookie cutter or a sharp knife to cut out circles slightly larger than the cavities of the mini muffin tin.
6. Place a spoonful of the caramelized apple mixture into each cavity of the mini muffin tin, filling them about halfway.
7. Carefully place a puff pastry circle on top of the apple mixture in each cavity, pressing down gently to seal the edges.
8. Bake in the preheated oven for 15-20 minutes, or until the pastry is golden brown and puffed up.
9. Remove from the oven and let the Tarte Tatin bites cool in the muffin tin for a few minutes.
10. Using a spoon, carefully loosen the edges of the Tarte Tatin bites and transfer them to a wire rack to cool completely.
11. Serve the Tarte Tatin bites warm or at room temperature, with whipped cream or vanilla ice cream on the side if desired. Dust with cinnamon or powdered sugar before serving, if desired.

These Tarte Tatin bites are a delicious and bite-sized version of the classic dessert, perfect for any occasion. Enjoy the caramelized apple goodness in every bite!

Asparagus Wrapped in Prosciutto

Ingredients:

- 1 bunch of asparagus (about 1 pound or 450g), tough ends trimmed
- 8 slices of prosciutto
- Olive oil, for drizzling
- Freshly ground black pepper, to taste
- Lemon wedges, for serving (optional)

Instructions:

1. Preheat your oven to 400°F (200°C). Line a baking sheet with parchment paper or aluminum foil.
2. Divide the asparagus spears into bundles, with about 4-5 spears per bundle.
3. Take a slice of prosciutto and wrap it tightly around each bundle of asparagus, starting from the bottom and working your way to the top. Repeat with the remaining asparagus spears and prosciutto slices.
4. Place the wrapped asparagus bundles on the prepared baking sheet, seam side down.
5. Drizzle the wrapped asparagus bundles with olive oil and sprinkle with freshly ground black pepper.
6. Bake in the preheated oven for 10-12 minutes, or until the asparagus is tender and the prosciutto is crispy.
7. Remove from the oven and let the asparagus bundles cool slightly before serving.
8. Optional: Serve the asparagus wrapped in prosciutto with lemon wedges on the side for squeezing over the top before eating.

These asparagus wrapped in prosciutto bundles are perfect as an appetizer or side dish for any occasion. Enjoy the delicious combination of flavors and textures in this simple and elegant dish!

Mussels in White Wine Sauce

Ingredients:

- 2 pounds of fresh mussels, cleaned and debearded
- 2 tablespoons of butter
- 2 cloves of garlic, minced
- 1 shallot, finely chopped
- 1 cup of dry white wine (such as Sauvignon Blanc or Pinot Grigio)
- 1/4 cup of chopped fresh parsley
- Salt and pepper to taste
- Crusty bread for serving

Instructions:

1. Clean the mussels under cold running water, scrubbing away any dirt or debris. Remove the beards by pulling them sharply towards the hinge of the shell. Discard any mussels that are open or cracked.
2. In a large pot or Dutch oven, melt the butter over medium heat. Add the minced garlic and chopped shallot, and sauté until softened and fragrant, about 2-3 minutes.
3. Pour in the white wine and bring it to a simmer.
4. Add the cleaned mussels to the pot and cover with a lid. Steam the mussels for 5-7 minutes, shaking the pot occasionally, until the mussels have opened.
5. Remove the lid and discard any mussels that have not opened.
6. Stir in the chopped parsley and season the sauce with salt and pepper to taste.
7. Serve the mussels hot with plenty of the white wine sauce, along with crusty bread for soaking up the delicious juices.

Enjoy your mussels in white wine sauce!

Pissaladière Bites (Mini French Onion Tart)

Ingredients:

For the dough:

- 1 sheet of puff pastry, thawed if frozen
- All-purpose flour for dusting

For the onion topping:

- 2 large onions, thinly sliced
- 2 tablespoons of olive oil
- 1 teaspoon of dried thyme
- Salt and pepper to taste

For assembling:

- 1/4 cup of black olives, pitted and sliced
- 6-8 anchovy fillets (optional)
- Fresh thyme leaves for garnish (optional)

Instructions:

1. Preheat your oven to 400°F (200°C). Line a baking sheet with parchment paper.
2. Roll out the puff pastry on a lightly floured surface to about 1/8 inch thickness. Using a cookie cutter or a knife, cut the puff pastry into small circles or squares, about 2-3 inches in diameter. Place the pastry shapes on the prepared baking sheet.
3. In a skillet, heat the olive oil over medium heat. Add the thinly sliced onions and cook, stirring occasionally, until they are caramelized and golden brown, about 20-25 minutes. Stir in the dried thyme and season with salt and pepper to taste.
4. Spoon a small amount of the caramelized onions onto each puff pastry round, leaving a small border around the edges.

5. If using, top each tart with a slice of black olive and an anchovy fillet.
6. Bake the pissaladière bites in the preheated oven for 15-20 minutes, or until the pastry is golden brown and crispy.
7. Remove from the oven and let cool slightly. Garnish with fresh thyme leaves, if desired, before serving.

These mini French onion tarts are best served warm as an appetizer or snack. Enjoy!

Chicken Liver Crostini with Caramelized Onions

Ingredients:

For the crostini:

- Baguette or ciabatta bread, sliced into thin rounds
- Olive oil
- Salt and pepper

For the chicken liver pâté:

- 1 pound of chicken livers, cleaned and trimmed
- 1 onion, finely chopped
- 2 cloves of garlic, minced
- 1/4 cup of brandy or cognac
- 1/2 cup of chicken broth
- 2 tablespoons of butter
- Salt and pepper to taste
- Fresh parsley or thyme for garnish (optional)

For the caramelized onions:

- 2 large onions, thinly sliced
- 2 tablespoons of olive oil
- 1 tablespoon of balsamic vinegar
- Salt and pepper to taste

Instructions:

1. Preheat your oven to 375°F (190°C). Place the bread slices on a baking sheet, brush them lightly with olive oil, and season with salt and pepper. Bake in the preheated oven for 8-10 minutes, or until golden and crispy. Set aside.
2. To make the chicken liver pâté, heat a skillet over medium-high heat. Add the chicken livers and cook for 3-4 minutes on each side, or until browned but still pink in the center. Remove from the skillet and set aside.
3. In the same skillet, add the chopped onion and garlic. Cook until softened and translucent, about 5 minutes.

4. Deglaze the skillet with brandy or cognac, scraping up any browned bits from the bottom of the pan. Allow the alcohol to cook off for a minute or two.
5. Add the chicken broth and cooked chicken livers back to the skillet. Cook for another 5-7 minutes, or until the livers are cooked through.
6. Transfer the mixture to a food processor and add the butter. Blend until smooth and creamy. Season with salt and pepper to taste.
7. For the caramelized onions, heat olive oil in a separate skillet over medium heat. Add the thinly sliced onions and cook, stirring occasionally, until they are caramelized and golden brown, about 20-25 minutes.
8. Stir in the balsamic vinegar and continue cooking for another 5 minutes. Season with salt and pepper to taste.
9. To assemble the crostini, spread a spoonful of the chicken liver pâté onto each toasted bread slice. Top with a dollop of caramelized onions.
10. Garnish with fresh parsley or thyme, if desired, and serve immediately.

These chicken liver crostini with caramelized onions are sure to impress your guests as a sophisticated appetizer or hors d'oeuvre. Enjoy!

Mini Quiche Lorraine

Ingredients:

For the pastry crust:

- 1 1/4 cups all-purpose flour
- 1/2 teaspoon salt
- 1/2 cup cold unsalted butter, cut into small cubes
- 1/4 cup ice water

For the filling:

- 6 slices bacon, cooked until crispy and crumbled
- 1 cup grated Gruyère cheese
- 3 large eggs
- 1 cup heavy cream
- 1/4 teaspoon salt
- 1/4 teaspoon black pepper
- Pinch of nutmeg
- Chopped fresh chives for garnish (optional)

Instructions:

1. Preheat your oven to 375°F (190°C). Lightly grease a mini muffin tin or line it with paper liners.
2. To make the pastry crust, in a food processor, combine the flour and salt. Add the cold butter cubes and pulse until the mixture resembles coarse crumbs.
3. Gradually add the ice water, 1 tablespoon at a time, and pulse until the dough comes together. Be careful not to overmix.
4. Turn the dough out onto a lightly floured surface and knead it gently until it forms a smooth ball. Wrap the dough in plastic wrap and refrigerate for at least 30 minutes.

5. Once chilled, roll out the dough on a floured surface to about 1/8 inch thickness. Use a round cookie cutter or the rim of a glass to cut out circles slightly larger than the size of the mini muffin cups.
6. Press each circle of dough into the prepared muffin tin, forming mini pastry shells.
7. In a bowl, whisk together the eggs, heavy cream, salt, pepper, and nutmeg until well combined.
8. Divide the crumbled bacon and grated Gruyère cheese evenly among the pastry shells.
9. Carefully pour the egg mixture into each pastry shell, filling them almost to the top.
10. Bake the mini quiches in the preheated oven for 15-20 minutes, or until the pastry is golden brown and the filling is set.
11. Remove from the oven and let cool in the muffin tin for a few minutes before transferring them to a wire rack to cool completely.
12. Garnish with chopped fresh chives, if desired, before serving.

These Mini Quiche Lorraine are perfect for brunch, parties, or as a savory snack any time of day. Enjoy!

Tuna Tartare with Avocado

Ingredients:

- 8 ounces sushi-grade tuna, finely diced
- 1 ripe avocado, diced
- 2 tablespoons red onion, finely minced
- 2 tablespoons fresh cilantro, chopped
- 1 tablespoon soy sauce
- 1 tablespoon sesame oil
- 1 tablespoon lime juice
- 1 teaspoon sriracha sauce (optional)
- Salt and pepper to taste
- Sesame seeds for garnish
- Tortilla chips or crispy wonton wrappers for serving

Instructions:

1. In a mixing bowl, combine the diced tuna, diced avocado, minced red onion, and chopped cilantro.
2. In a separate small bowl, whisk together the soy sauce, sesame oil, lime juice, and sriracha sauce (if using).
3. Pour the dressing over the tuna and avocado mixture, and gently toss until everything is evenly coated. Season with salt and pepper to taste.
4. Cover the bowl with plastic wrap and refrigerate for at least 30 minutes to allow the flavors to meld together.
5. Just before serving, give the tuna tartare a final toss to redistribute the dressing.
6. To serve, spoon the tuna tartare into small bowls or onto a platter. Garnish with sesame seeds and additional chopped cilantro, if desired.
7. Serve the tuna tartare with tortilla chips or crispy wonton wrappers on the side for scooping.

Enjoy this delicious tuna tartare with avocado as a light appetizer or a stylish starter for your next meal!

Cherry Tomato and Mozzarella Skewers

Ingredients:

- Cherry tomatoes
- Fresh mozzarella balls (bocconcini)
- Fresh basil leaves
- Balsamic glaze (optional)
- Olive oil
- Salt and pepper, to taste
- Wooden skewers

Instructions:

1. If you're using wooden skewers, soak them in water for about 30 minutes to prevent them from burning on the grill or in the oven.
2. Rinse the cherry tomatoes and pat them dry with a paper towel. Similarly, drain the mozzarella balls if they are packed in liquid.
3. Assemble the skewers by threading a cherry tomato, a mozzarella ball, and a fresh basil leaf onto each skewer. Repeat until all ingredients are used, alternating the components as desired.
4. Once all the skewers are assembled, arrange them on a serving platter or tray.
5. Drizzle the skewers with a little olive oil and sprinkle with salt and pepper to taste. Optionally, you can also drizzle with balsamic glaze for extra flavor.
6. Serve the cherry tomato and mozzarella skewers immediately, or refrigerate them until ready to serve.

These skewers are not only visually appealing but also bursting with fresh flavors.

They're sure to be a hit at your next gathering!

Duck Confit Crostini with Cherry Compote

Ingredients:

For the duck confit:

- 2 duck legs (confit legs if available)
- Salt and pepper
- 2 cloves of garlic, crushed
- 4 sprigs of fresh thyme
- Duck fat (enough to cover the duck legs)

For the cherry compote:

- 2 cups fresh cherries, pitted and halved
- 1/4 cup granulated sugar
- 2 tablespoons red wine vinegar
- Pinch of salt

For the crostini:

- Baguette, sliced into thin rounds
- Olive oil
- Salt and pepper

Instructions:

1. Preheat your oven to 300°F (150°C).
2. Season the duck legs generously with salt and pepper. Place them in a baking dish along with the crushed garlic and fresh thyme.
3. Pour duck fat over the duck legs until they are completely submerged. If you don't have enough duck fat, you can supplement with olive oil.
4. Cover the baking dish with foil and transfer it to the preheated oven. Cook for about 2-3 hours, or until the duck is tender and easily pulls away from the bone.

5. While the duck is cooking, make the cherry compote. In a saucepan, combine the cherries, sugar, red wine vinegar, and a pinch of salt. Cook over medium heat, stirring occasionally, until the cherries are soft and the mixture has thickened slightly, about 10-15 minutes. Remove from heat and let cool.
6. Once the duck is cooked, remove it from the oven and let it cool slightly. Then, shred the meat from the bones and set aside.
7. Increase the oven temperature to 375°F (190°C). Arrange the baguette slices on a baking sheet in a single layer. Brush each slice with olive oil and sprinkle with salt and pepper.
8. Bake the crostini in the preheated oven for 8-10 minutes, or until golden brown and crispy.
9. To assemble the crostini, top each slice of toasted baguette with a spoonful of shredded duck confit, followed by a spoonful of cherry compote.
10. Serve the duck confit crostini with cherry compote immediately, garnished with fresh thyme or microgreens if desired.

These duck confit crostini with cherry compote are sure to impress your guests with their combination of flavors and textures. Enjoy!

Smoked Salmon Blinis

Ingredients:

For the blinis:

- 1 cup all-purpose flour
- 1 teaspoon baking powder
- 1/2 teaspoon salt
- 1 cup milk
- 1 large egg
- 2 tablespoons unsalted butter, melted
- Cooking spray or additional butter for cooking

For serving:

- Smoked salmon slices
- Cream cheese or crème fraîche
- Fresh dill or chives, for garnish
- Lemon wedges, for serving

Instructions:

1. In a large mixing bowl, whisk together the flour, baking powder, and salt.
2. In a separate bowl, whisk together the milk, egg, and melted butter until well combined.
3. Pour the wet ingredients into the dry ingredients and whisk until just combined. Be careful not to overmix; a few lumps are okay.
4. Let the batter rest for about 10 minutes while you preheat your skillet or griddle.
5. Heat a non-stick skillet or griddle over medium heat and lightly coat with cooking spray or butter.
6. Once the skillet is hot, drop small spoonfuls of batter onto the skillet to form mini pancakes (about 2 inches in diameter).

7. Cook the blinis for 1-2 minutes on each side, or until golden brown and cooked through. You may need to adjust the heat as necessary to prevent them from burning.
8. Transfer the cooked blinis to a plate and repeat with the remaining batter, adding more cooking spray or butter to the skillet as needed.
9. To serve, top each blini with a small dollop of cream cheese or crème fraîche, followed by a slice of smoked salmon.
10. Garnish with fresh dill or chives, and serve with lemon wedges on the side for squeezing over the salmon.

These smoked salmon blinis make a delicious appetizer or hors d'oeuvre for any occasion. Enjoy!

Cheese and Herb Soufflés

Ingredients:

- 3 tablespoons unsalted butter, plus extra for greasing the ramekins
- 3 tablespoons all-purpose flour
- 1 cup milk
- 1/2 teaspoon salt
- 1/4 teaspoon black pepper
- Pinch of cayenne pepper (optional)
- 1 cup grated cheese (such as Gruyère, cheddar, or Parmesan)
- 4 large eggs, separated
- 2 tablespoons finely chopped fresh herbs (such as parsley, chives, or thyme)
- Extra grated cheese for topping (optional)

Instructions:

1. Preheat your oven to 375°F (190°C). Grease four 1-cup ramekins generously with butter and sprinkle with grated cheese, if using. This will help the soufflés rise and give them a nice crust.
2. In a saucepan, melt the butter over medium heat. Add the flour and whisk continuously for 1-2 minutes to cook the flour and form a roux.
3. Gradually whisk in the milk, a little at a time, until smooth and well combined. Cook the mixture, stirring constantly, until it thickens and comes to a simmer.
4. Remove the saucepan from the heat and stir in the salt, black pepper, cayenne pepper (if using), and grated cheese until the cheese is melted and the mixture is smooth. Let it cool slightly.
5. Once the cheese mixture has cooled, whisk in the egg yolks one at a time until fully incorporated. Stir in the chopped fresh herbs.
6. In a clean, dry bowl, beat the egg whites with an electric mixer until stiff peaks form.
7. Gently fold one-third of the beaten egg whites into the cheese mixture to lighten it. Then, carefully fold in the remaining egg whites until no streaks remain, being careful not to deflate the mixture.
8. Divide the soufflé mixture evenly among the prepared ramekins, filling them almost to the top.

9. Place the ramekins on a baking sheet and bake in the preheated oven for 18-20 minutes, or until the soufflés are puffed up and golden brown on top.
10. Serve the cheese and herb soufflés immediately, as they will begin to deflate shortly after coming out of the oven.

These cheese and herb soufflés make an elegant and flavorful appetizer or side dish for any meal. Enjoy the light and fluffy texture along with the savory cheese and aromatic herbs!

Bouillabaisse Shooters

Ingredients:

For the bouillabaisse:

- 1 lb mixed seafood (such as shrimp, mussels, clams, and white fish fillets), cleaned and deveined
- 2 tablespoons olive oil
- 1 onion, chopped
- 2 cloves garlic, minced
- 1 fennel bulb, thinly sliced
- 1 leek, thinly sliced
- 1 carrot, peeled and diced
- 1 celery stalk, diced
- 1 can (14 oz) diced tomatoes
- 4 cups fish or seafood broth
- 1/2 cup dry white wine
- 1 teaspoon saffron threads
- 2 bay leaves
- Salt and pepper to taste
- Fresh parsley, chopped, for garnish

For serving:

- Shot glasses or small cups
- Baguette slices, toasted
- Rouille (optional, for garnish)

Instructions:

1. In a large pot, heat the olive oil over medium heat. Add the chopped onion and minced garlic, and sauté until softened and fragrant, about 2-3 minutes.
2. Add the sliced fennel, leek, carrot, and celery to the pot. Cook, stirring occasionally, until the vegetables are tender, about 5 minutes.

3. Stir in the diced tomatoes, fish or seafood broth, white wine, saffron threads, and bay leaves. Bring the mixture to a simmer.
4. Once simmering, add the mixed seafood to the pot. Cook until the seafood is cooked through and the mussels and clams have opened, about 5-7 minutes. Discard any mussels or clams that do not open.
5. Season the bouillabaisse with salt and pepper to taste. Remove the bay leaves.
6. Ladle the bouillabaisse into shot glasses or small cups, filling them about halfway.
7. Garnish each bouillabaisse shooter with chopped fresh parsley.
8. Serve the bouillabaisse shooters with toasted baguette slices on the side for dipping. Optionally, you can also serve with a dollop of rouille on top of the baguette slices.

These bouillabaisse shooters are perfect for entertaining, allowing your guests to enjoy the flavors of this classic French dish in a fun and elegant presentation. Enjoy!

Mushroom and Leek Quiche

Ingredients:

For the crust:

- 1 1/4 cups all-purpose flour
- 1/2 teaspoon salt
- 1/2 cup cold unsalted butter, cut into small cubes
- 3-4 tablespoons ice water

For the filling:

- 1 tablespoon olive oil
- 2 leeks, white and light green parts only, thinly sliced
- 8 ounces mushrooms (such as cremini or button), sliced
- 2 cloves garlic, minced
- 1 teaspoon fresh thyme leaves
- Salt and pepper to taste
- 4 large eggs
- 1 cup milk or heavy cream
- 1 cup grated Gruyère or Swiss cheese

Instructions:

1. Preheat your oven to 375°F (190°C).
2. To make the crust, in a food processor, combine the flour and salt. Add the cold butter cubes and pulse until the mixture resembles coarse crumbs.
3. Gradually add the ice water, 1 tablespoon at a time, and pulse until the dough comes together. Be careful not to overmix; the dough should hold together when pinched.
4. Turn the dough out onto a lightly floured surface and shape it into a disk. Wrap the dough in plastic wrap and refrigerate for at least 30 minutes.
5. Once chilled, roll out the dough on a floured surface to fit a 9-inch tart or quiche pan. Press the dough into the bottom and sides of the pan, trimming any excess dough. Prick the bottom of the crust with a fork.

6. Line the crust with parchment paper and fill it with pie weights or dried beans. Blind bake the crust in the preheated oven for 15 minutes. Remove the parchment paper and weights, and bake for an additional 5 minutes, or until lightly golden. Remove from the oven and set aside.
7. While the crust is baking, prepare the filling. Heat the olive oil in a skillet over medium heat. Add the sliced leeks and cook until softened, about 5 minutes.
8. Add the sliced mushrooms, minced garlic, and fresh thyme leaves to the skillet. Cook, stirring occasionally, until the mushrooms are tender and any liquid has evaporated, about 8-10 minutes. Season with salt and pepper to taste.
9. In a mixing bowl, whisk together the eggs and milk or heavy cream until well combined.
10. Spread the cooked mushroom and leek mixture evenly over the bottom of the pre-baked crust. Sprinkle grated cheese over the top.
11. Pour the egg mixture over the filling in the crust.
12. Bake the quiche in the preheated oven for 30-35 minutes, or until the filling is set and the top is golden brown.
13. Remove from the oven and let cool slightly before slicing and serving.

Enjoy your mushroom and leek quiche warm or at room temperature, as a delicious and satisfying meal!

Chicken Liver Mousse with Port Wine Gelée

Ingredients:

For the chicken liver mousse:

- 1 lb chicken livers, trimmed and cleaned
- 1 onion, finely chopped
- 2 cloves garlic, minced
- 1/4 cup brandy or cognac
- 1/2 cup heavy cream
- 4 tablespoons unsalted butter
- Salt and pepper to taste
- Pinch of nutmeg
- Fresh thyme leaves for garnish (optional)

For the port wine gelée:

- 1 cup port wine
- 1/4 cup water
- 1/4 cup sugar
- 2 teaspoons powdered gelatin

Instructions:

1. Start by making the chicken liver mousse. In a skillet, melt 2 tablespoons of butter over medium heat. Add the chopped onion and minced garlic, and cook until softened and translucent, about 5 minutes.
2. Add the cleaned chicken livers to the skillet and cook until they are browned on the outside but still pink on the inside, about 5-7 minutes.
3. Remove the skillet from the heat and carefully add the brandy or cognac. Return the skillet to the heat and cook for another 2-3 minutes, allowing the alcohol to cook off.

4. Transfer the cooked chicken livers, onions, and garlic to a food processor. Add the heavy cream and remaining 2 tablespoons of butter. Season with salt, pepper, and a pinch of nutmeg.
5. Blend the mixture until smooth and creamy. Taste and adjust seasoning if necessary.
6. Transfer the chicken liver mousse to small serving dishes or ramekins. Smooth the tops with a spatula.
7. Cover the dishes with plastic wrap and refrigerate for at least 2 hours, or until the mousse is set.
8. While the mousse is chilling, make the port wine gelée. In a small saucepan, combine the port wine, water, and sugar. Heat over medium heat, stirring occasionally, until the sugar has dissolved.
9. In a separate bowl, sprinkle the powdered gelatin over 1/4 cup of cold water. Let it sit for a few minutes to soften.
10. Once the gelatin has softened, add it to the warm port wine mixture and stir until completely dissolved.
11. Remove the saucepan from the heat and let the mixture cool slightly.
12. Carefully pour the port wine gelée over the chilled chicken liver mousse in each dish, covering the top completely.
13. Return the dishes to the refrigerator and chill for an additional 1-2 hours, or until the gelée is set.
14. Before serving, garnish the chicken liver mousse with fresh thyme leaves, if desired.

Enjoy your chicken liver mousse with port wine gelée as a sophisticated appetizer, served with toasted bread or crackers!

Sardine Pâté on Baguette

Ingredients:

For the sardine pâté:

- 2 cans (3.75 oz each) of sardines in oil, drained
- 4 oz cream cheese, softened
- 2 tablespoons mayonnaise
- 1 tablespoon lemon juice
- 1 teaspoon Dijon mustard
- 2 cloves garlic, minced
- Salt and pepper to taste
- Fresh parsley or dill for garnish (optional)

For serving:

- Baguette, sliced into thin rounds
- Olive oil for brushing

Instructions:

1. In a food processor, combine the drained sardines, softened cream cheese, mayonnaise, lemon juice, Dijon mustard, minced garlic, salt, and pepper.
2. Pulse the mixture until smooth and creamy, scraping down the sides of the bowl as needed.
3. Taste the pâté and adjust seasoning if necessary.
4. Transfer the sardine pâté to a serving bowl and refrigerate for at least 30 minutes to allow the flavors to meld together.
5. While the pâté is chilling, preheat your oven to 375°F (190°C).
6. Arrange the baguette slices on a baking sheet in a single layer. Brush each slice lightly with olive oil.
7. Bake the baguette slices in the preheated oven for 8-10 minutes, or until golden brown and crispy.
8. Remove the baguette slices from the oven and let them cool slightly.

9. Once the baguette slices are cooled, spread a generous amount of the chilled sardine pâté onto each slice.
10. Garnish the sardine pâté on baguette with fresh parsley or dill, if desired.
11. Serve immediately as an appetizer or snack.

Enjoy your sardine pâté on baguette as a tasty and satisfying treat!

Cucumber Cups with Crab Salad

Ingredients:

For the cucumber cups:

- 2 large English cucumbers
- Salt

For the crab salad:

- 8 oz lump crab meat, picked over for shells
- 1/4 cup mayonnaise
- 1 tablespoon lemon juice
- 1 teaspoon Dijon mustard
- 1 green onion, finely chopped
- 1 tablespoon finely chopped fresh dill
- Salt and pepper to taste

For garnish:

- Fresh dill sprigs
- Lemon wedges

Instructions:

1. Start by preparing the cucumber cups. Peel the cucumbers and slice them into rounds, each about 1 inch thick. Use a melon baller or a small spoon to scoop out the seeds from the center of each cucumber slice, creating a small cup. Place the cucumber cups on a paper towel-lined plate and sprinkle them lightly with salt. Let them sit for about 10 minutes to draw out excess moisture.
2. While the cucumber cups are draining, prepare the crab salad. In a mixing bowl, combine the lump crab meat, mayonnaise, lemon juice, Dijon mustard, chopped

green onion, and chopped fresh dill. Gently fold the ingredients together until well combined. Season with salt and pepper to taste.
3. Pat the cucumber cups dry with paper towels to remove any excess moisture.
4. Fill each cucumber cup with a spoonful of the crab salad, mounding it slightly.
5. Garnish the filled cucumber cups with fresh dill sprigs and lemon wedges.
6. Arrange the cucumber cups on a serving platter and serve immediately.

These cucumber cups with crab salad are best enjoyed fresh, so assemble them just before serving. They make an elegant and flavorful appetizer that's sure to impress your guests!

Salmon Tartare with Dill and Capers

Ingredients:

- 8 oz sushi-grade salmon, skinless and boneless, finely diced
- 2 tablespoons capers, drained and chopped
- 2 tablespoons fresh dill, chopped
- 1 tablespoon red onion, finely chopped
- 1 tablespoon lemon juice
- 1 tablespoon extra virgin olive oil
- Salt and pepper to taste
- Optional garnishes: additional capers, dill sprigs, lemon wedges, thinly sliced cucumber or radish, microgreens

Instructions:

1. In a mixing bowl, combine the diced salmon, chopped capers, chopped fresh dill, finely chopped red onion, lemon juice, and extra virgin olive oil.
2. Gently toss the ingredients together until well combined.
3. Season the salmon tartare with salt and pepper to taste. Remember that capers are naturally salty, so adjust the seasoning accordingly.
4. Taste the tartare and adjust the seasoning or add more lemon juice, olive oil, or dill if desired.
5. To serve, divide the salmon tartare among individual serving dishes or arrange it on a platter.
6. If desired, garnish the salmon tartare with additional capers, dill sprigs, lemon wedges, thinly sliced cucumber or radish, or microgreens.
7. Serve the salmon tartare immediately with crackers, toasted baguette slices, or crostini.

Enjoy the fresh and vibrant flavors of this salmon tartare with dill and capers as a sophisticated appetizer or light meal!

www.ingramcontent.com/pod-product-compliance
Lightning Source LLC
LaVergne TN
LVHW062047070526
838201LV00080B/2160